Flowers of Grass

Flowers of Grass

SEAN EWING

RESOURCE *Publications* • Eugene, Oregon

FLOWERS OF GRASS

Resource Publications
An Imprint of Wipf and Stock Publishers
199 W. 8th Ave., Suite 3
Eugene, OR 97401

www.wipfandstock.com

PAPERBACK ISBN: 978–1-6667-4292–3
HARDCOVER ISBN: 978–1-6667-4293–0
EBOOK ISBN: 978–1-6667-4294–7

MAY 2, 2022 10:29 AM

CONTENTS

List of Images | *v*

Preface | *viii*

Lament | 2

Heartache | 4

Shadow | 6

For Ashley and Laura | 8

Faithful | 10

Having Been Broken | 12

Unwilling | 14

Chains | 16

Formed | 18

Two Worlds | 21

Grave | 23

Whisper | 25

Take | 28

Flowers of Grass | 30

Sojourner | 33

Without You | 35

Delusion | 37

Yours | 39

Lament #2 | 41

Confess | 43

Until | 45

Journey | 47

Nights so Dark | 49

Reflect | 51

That Day | 53

Struggle | 58

Morning | 60

Worth | 62

Turn | 64

Watch | 66

Hesitate | 68

Break | 70

Faint | 72

Live | 74

Rose | 76

LIST OF IMAGES

All images digitally enhanced by Sean Ewing

1. **That Day** – Base image - https://pixabay.com/photos/people-shadow-dark-night-smoke-2574169/

2. **Shadow** - Base image https://pixabay.com/photos/woman-girl-lady-people-side-view-2607804/

3. **For Ashley and Laura** – Base image https://pixabay.com/photos/baby-parenthood-hand-finger-mother-1271742/

4. **Faithful** – Base image https://pixabay.com/photos/cross-wooden-cross-symbol-4586577/

5. **Heartache** – Base image https://pixabay.com/photos/alone-to-be-alone-archetype-513525/

6. **Having Been Broken** – Base image https://www.pexels.com/photo/close-up-shot-of-shards-of-a-broken-ceramic-plate-on-a-wooden-surface-6717606/

7. **Unwilling** – Base image https://pixabay.com/photos/crying-tears-sadness-depression-4577567/>

8. **Chains** – Base image https://pixabay.com/photos/chains-feet-sand-bondage-prison-19176/

9. **Formed** – Base mage https://pixabay.com/photos/forge-craft-hot-to-form-iron-550622/

10. **Two Worlds** - Base image https://pixabay.com/photos/forest-trail-fork-in-the-road-path-6607631/

11. **Grave** - Base image https://pixabay.com/photos/angel-woman-head-face-figure-2899333/

12. **Whisper** - Base image https://pixabay.com/photos/ angel-whisper-christmas-1402789/

13. **Take** - Base image https://pixabay.com/photos/ climbing-hands-socket-grab-6123693/

14. **Flowers of Grass** – Base image Lisa Fotios from Pexels

15. **Sojourner** - Base image https://pixabay.com/photos/ path-rural-nature-road-countryside-6567149/

16. **Without You** - Base image https://pixabay.com/photos/ man-fog-silhouette-kneeling-kneel-1868418/

17. **Delusion** - Base image https://pixabay.com/photos/ statue-churchyard-memorial-praying-364524/

18. **Yours** – Base image https://pixabay.com/photos/ bird-dove-flying-dove-flying-bird-4062359/

19. **Lament** - Base image https://pixabay.com/photos/ morning-girl-beautiful-femininity-1369446/

20. **Lament #2** - Base image https://pixabay.com/photos/ angel-woman-head-face-figure-2899333/

21. **Confess** - Image by Sean Ewing

22. **Until** - Base image https://pixabay.com/users/ jplenio-7645255/?tab=ec&pagi=3

23. **Journey** - Base image https://www.pexels.com/photo/ red-leaf-trees-near-the-road-33109/

24. **Nights So Dark** - Base image https://pixabay.com/photos/ alley-street-night-evening-city-89197/

25. **Reflect** - Base image https://www.pexels.com/photo/ backlit-beach-clouds-dark-289998/

26. **Struggle** – Base image https://pixabay.com/photos/ drowning-man-sea-hands-5654815/

27. **Morning** - Base image https://pixabay.com/photos/ grasses-sea-sunset-sunrise-sun-1046475/

28. **Worth** – Base image https://pxhere.com/en/photo/490935

29. **Turn** – Base image https://www.pexels.com/photo/ an-elderly-man-looking-outside-a-window-8172564/

30. **Watch** – Base image Jan Koetsier from Pexels https://www.pexels.com/photo/window-with-broken-glass-2724373/

31. **Hesitate** - Base image https://pixabay.com/photos/feet-legs-standing-waiting-349687/

32. **Break** – Base image https://www.pexels.com/photo/crop-preoccupied-woman-frowning-and-crying-unhappily-5537882/

33. **Faint** - Base image https://pixabay.com/photos/replacement-lamp-light-lighting-1116873/

34. **Live** - Base image https://pixabay.com/photos/god-jesus-jesus-christ-easter-2012104/

35. **Inside page** - Base image https://pixabay.com/photos/virgin-mary-statue-cemetery-5756165/

36. **Rose** – Image by Sean Ewing

PREFACE

How long, oh Lord, how long?

Will you forget me forever?

How long will you hide your face from me?

My God, my God, why have you forsaken me?

To LAMENT IS TO express deep regret, grief, or sorrow. The above questions are questions David asked in his laments. How do we today ask these types of questions? How do we lament and do it biblically? The book of Psalms in the Bible provides us many examples. Approximately one third of the psalms are in the category of lament. Common themes we see in lamenting psalms are mockery, slander by personal enemies, warfare, sin, and guilt.

Lament psalms follow a form consisting of several elements. These elements can occur in any sequence and can occur more than once. The lament typically begins with an invocation or introductory cry to God and sometimes already containing the second element of complaint. The complaint is the definition of the crisis or situation and the reason for the lament, the thing that the poet is responding to. In the element of petition the poet describes what is being asked of God to remedy the distressing issue(s). Most lament psalms contain a statement of confidence in God, a praise to God. These lamenting psalms thus contain a reversal or even a recantation: the poet begins saying it's hopeless and ends with confidence in God.

In addition to the afore mentioned elements there can be a strong sense of protest or even chastisement of God for not having corrected whatever the situation is. The sense of outrage is combined with statements of faith in God who in his sovereignty orchestrates all human affairs and is a friend of the sorrowful and oppressed. This is what makes it biblical, a biblical lament has a pivot to an already existing confidence and faith in God. There are many laments in our world that bemoan life and struggle but never turn to God.

There are other scriptures outside of the psalms that contain lament. The Bible records that God also laments! He does so over the sin and dis-obedience of his people referenced in Genesis 6:6. He lamented the de-struction of his perfect world and continuing rebellion and sin that keeps it in bondage. The book of Jeremiah tells us about God's sorrow over the desolation of his chosen land, Israel (Jeremiah 12:20–21). The book of Lamentations records the despair and dismay experienced by the nation of Judah in her defeat to the Babylonians in 586 B.C. Jesus grieved and used lament when he was on the earth. The scene when Lazarus died, his sisters Mary and Martha grieved, and their friends lamented over this loss (John 11:17–37). Jesus' heart was touched to such an extent that he wept along with them (John 11:35).

What follows in this book is poetry that laments and laments in a bib-lical sense. The poems follow the biblical design mentioned earlier with the key being a pivot to praise and honor God. Life is hard and we encounter many difficulties and sorrows. My prayer is that in reading the poems you can see the benefits and blessing of biblical lament. I know for me one of the blessings that lamenting has produced is an intimacy with God that I did not have before in my life.

The Bible instructs us to lament over our sin. This kind of lamentation is associated with repentance (Matthew 3:8; Acts 2:38; James 5:1). Repen-tance is understanding how bad our sin is against God and purposing (in the strength of the Lord) to turn away from it. When we see our sin the way God does, we should lament over it. I also pray that you can see Christ in all of this. And that our only true hope is hope in Christ our Redeemer who conquered death and sin when he was crucified and raised from the dead. Salvation is by no other name than Jesus (Acts 4:12). Praise God for his mercy, grace, and redemption in Christ.

Israel brought their lament to God in the psalms on the basis of his covenant with them. The same is true for us today in the new covenant in Christ. Lamenting is a pathway to intimacy with God. Our gracious God who calls us into relationship with him, lament is one of the ways we re-spond. Biblical lament is not simply an outlet for our frustrations, lament-ing is a form of prayer and praise to God. In the psalms the laments are calls for God to act. The cry is to God to be merciful and to act on their behalf. The psalms continue to provide us with examples of an intimate relationship with God and what that interaction looks like.

Lamenting is not our final prayer; it is a prayer in the here and now. We can end our laments in gratitude and thanks to God for his grace, mercy, and redemption in Christ. Because Jesus Christ died on a miserable cross for our sin and is risen from the dead, we know that misery, anguish, and sorrow is not how the story ends. Ultimately in Christ every tear is wiped away, death is swallowed up in victory, heaven and earth are made new and, believers in Christ rise in glorious bodies. Then instead of lamenting we will sing a great resounding "Hallelujah!"

March 2022
Sean Ewing

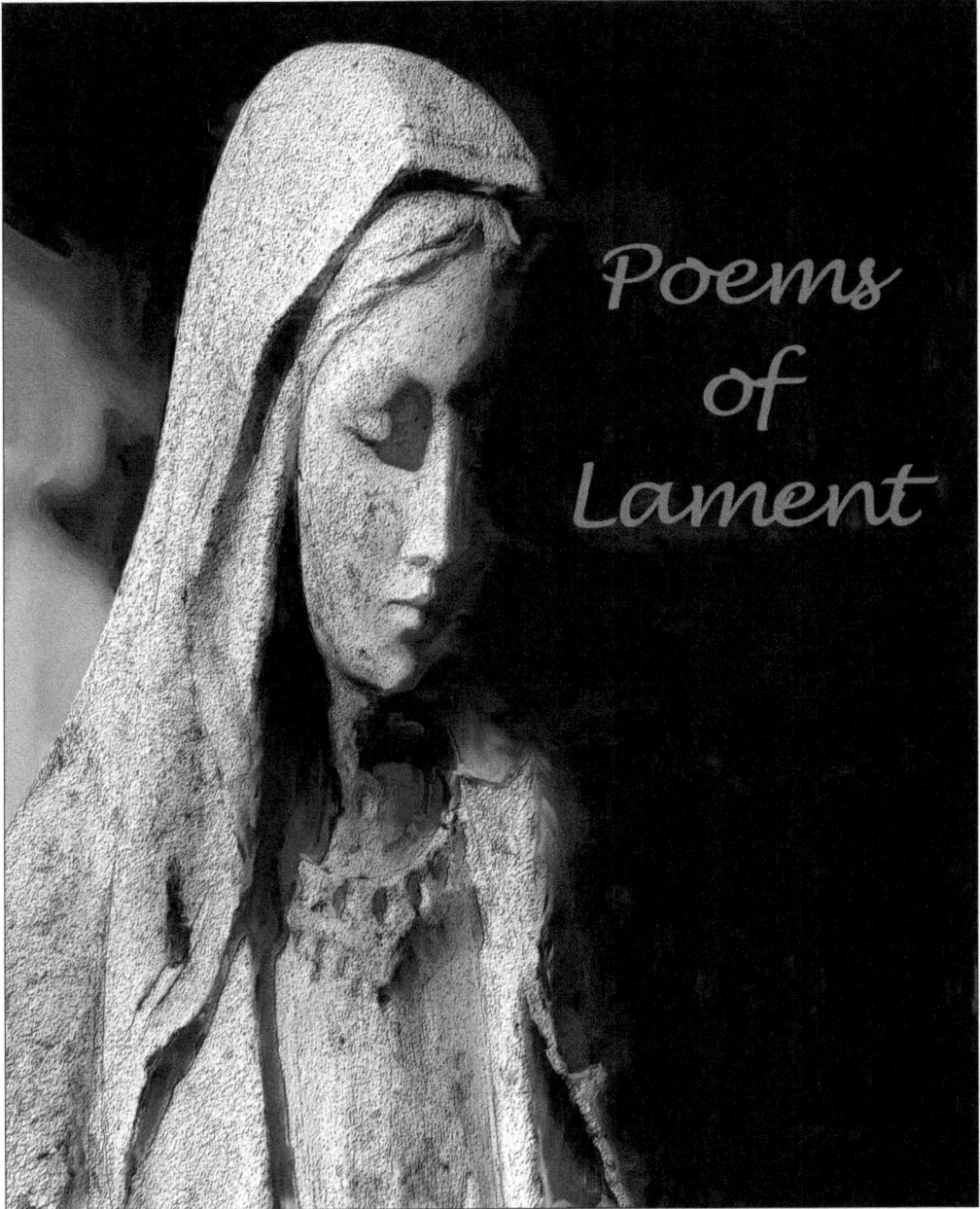

Poems
of
Lament

LAMENT

How can I endure this any longer?
Arms stretched out to You in anguish
The brokenness of this world
The frailty that lives inside me

I want You to take me away
I feel as though I'm dying inside
I know Your Word is truth
Oh Lord, help my unbelief

To be changed by Your gracious hand
May these afflictions change my heart

Help my frail heart to not forsake You
Lord use my life for Your honor
For Your purpose and kingdom
My struggles have emptied me before You

Lord, I surrender to You
Take what is Yours, my life, I offer it to You

Like a thick fog hugging the ground
It's hard to navigate life's veiled path
In my lament I desperately cry out to You
Do what is needed for me to be changed

When will sight be given to these weary eyes
Why do You hide Your face?
Is not my affliction obvious?
I don't want to fight this battle anymore
In this valley I wonder where God is

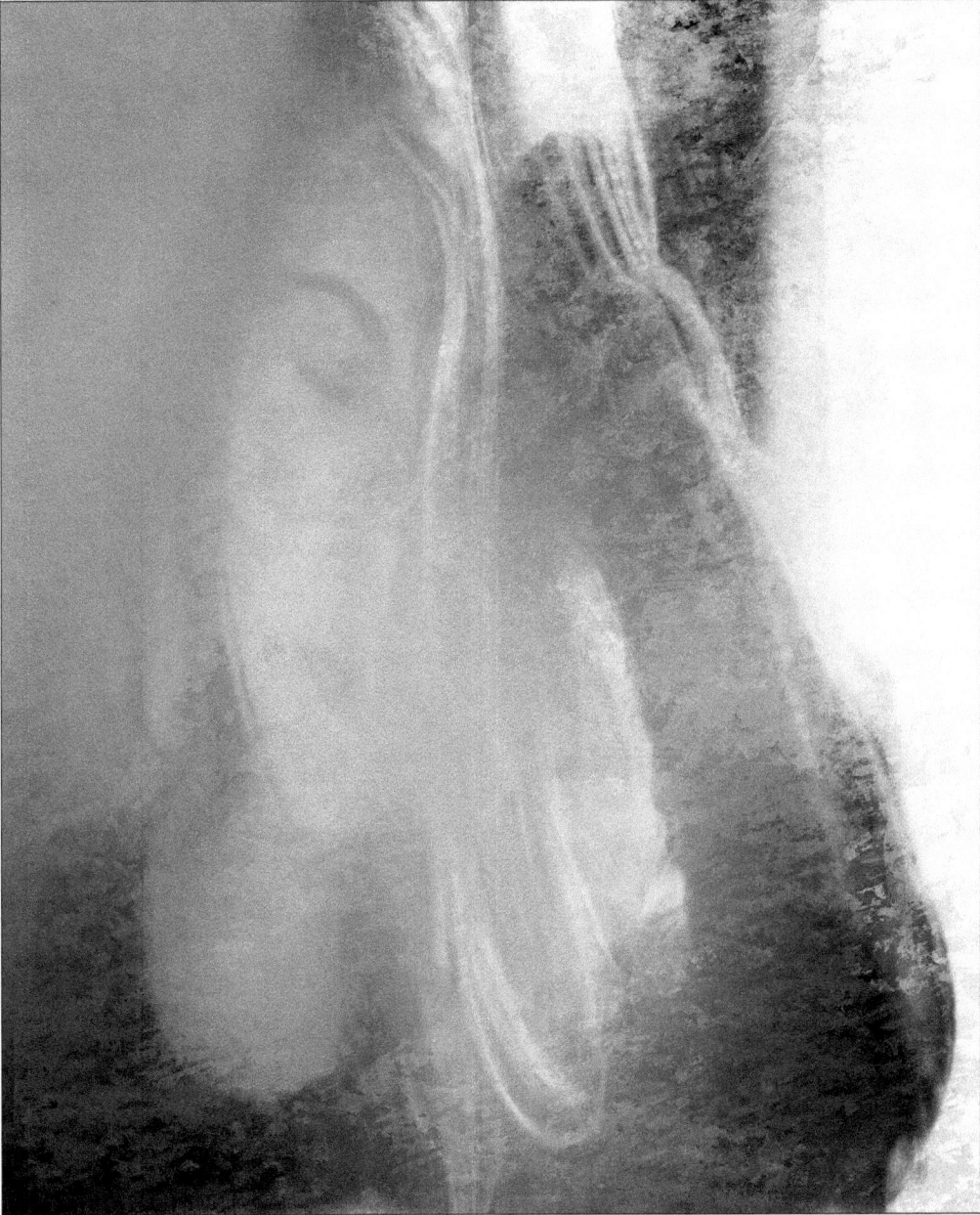

HEARTACHE

What a suffering piece of heartache
My life has turned out to be
It's been painful, learning the hard way

Looking back at the past, I recognize
The dark shadow of myself
It was God's grace that found me

A life of seeking sensual earthly things
Like sleeping on a bed of nails
Nothing much there but disappointment

It was a dying on the inside
In the clutches of a never-ending slide
Without Your grace Lord I would have died

My selfishness took its toll, it always slays
No longer the case these latter days
Your unfailing love has changed my ways

SHADOW

Shadow upon a rock
Something soft
On something hard
Rocky hard place
In a gentle shadow
Many times, in life
It can be like a rock
Hard, heavy, cold
But now I see that shadow
That heavy rock persists
But that shadow
Reminds me
I'm not alone
I know that in faith
The ever faithful One
Is that shadow on my rocky life
God is ever faithful

FOR ASHLEY AND LAURA

I was thrilled to see you born
I was so excited to be your father
I always wanted to be a good father
But I failed you in many ways
I truly meant to be faithful, strong, and true
To be there to comfort and love
Instead, you got your father's sin
I failed to live as Christ within
I was fighting demons in my life
I was struggling in sin
My beautiful daughters
I swam through rough waters
To get back, back, back to you
But it was too late
Forgive me for how I failed you
Not showing you how great God is
A father's sin is a terrible thing
All the fear and pain it can bring
I confess as your father I am a failure
I'm grateful though, for my Savior
That changed my heart and behavior
You endured the darkness of your father's sin
In forgiveness a new love can begin

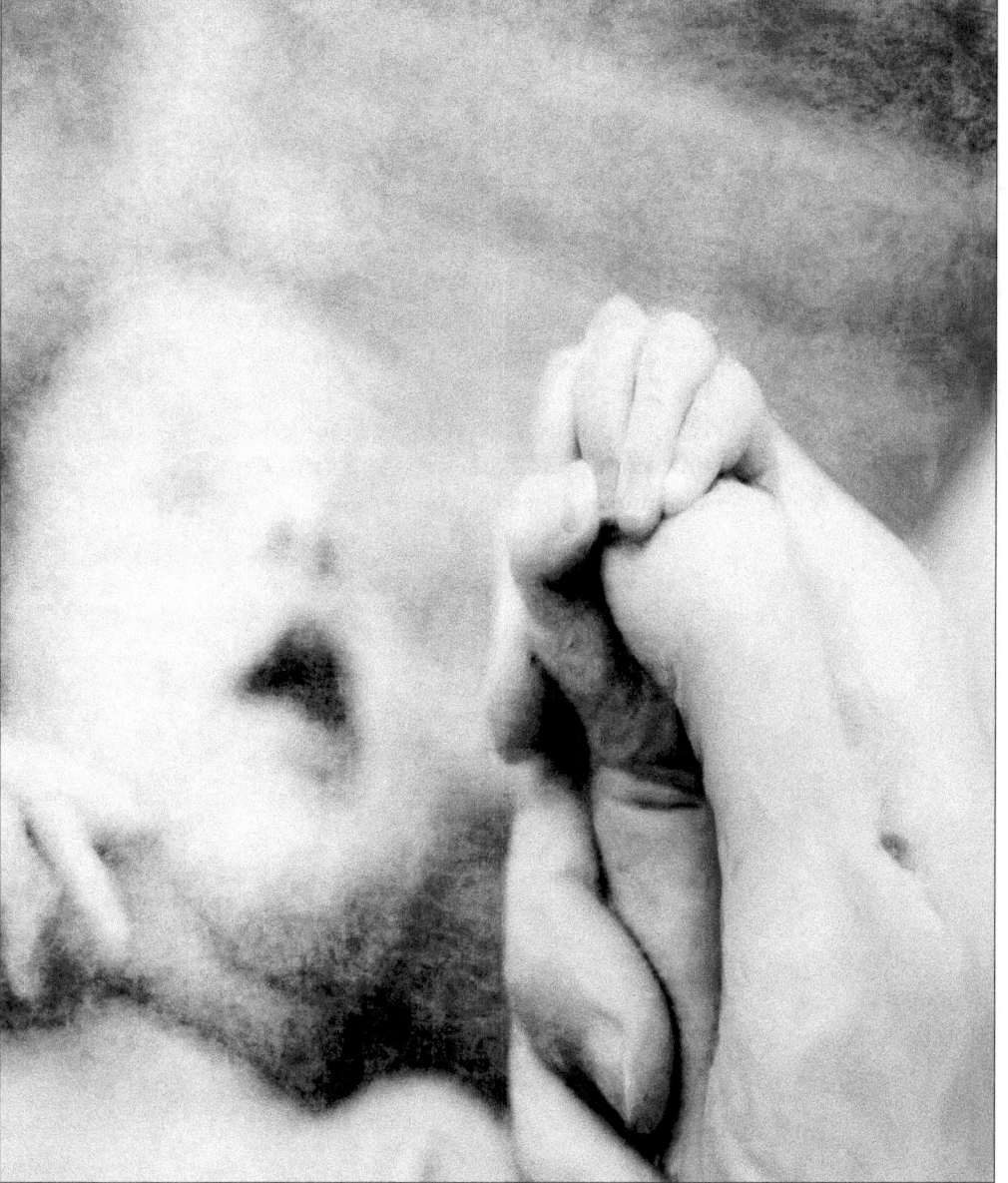

FAITHFUL

Lord, in the time of my life
Am I loving You and loving people?
Am I living truly for You?
Am I faithful in Your grace?
Am I all about You Lord?

In the life that You gave me
Do I surrender love of self to You?
Do I stand my ground in Your Word?
If today is the day You have appointed to take me
Was I faithful in the life that You gave?

At times in my life, I strayed from Your truth
At times in my life, I wondered into darkness
No more, Redeemer I follow only You
Today is a day for faithfulness to You
In this life that You gave me

HAVING BEEN BROKEN

The worst illness is one undetected
Slow subtle decay this cancer
The cancer of a prideful heart
Pride points to a greater fault
Ignoring what we have hidden
I used to be able to pretend
I can no longer hide
My pride inside
My deceit was displayed for all to see
The only thing that could have saved me
Was God's redemption in Christ
Only after having been broken
Looking up from the bottom
In God's grace I find the cure
And seeing my Savior so pure
Pride's deception removed now it's clear
To then realize my Jesus is so near
It's easy to believe you are nothing like me
Only salvation in Christ are we free

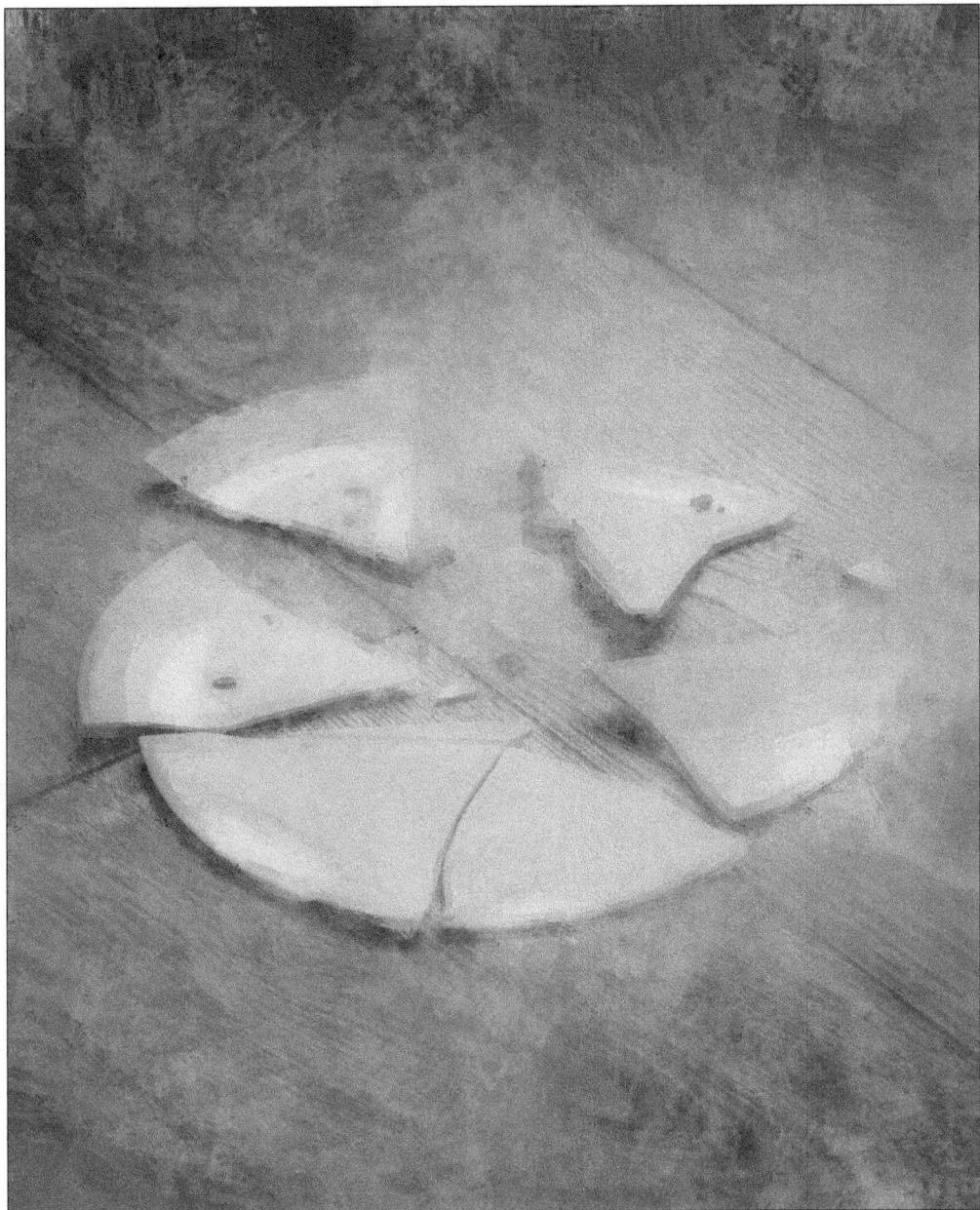

UNWILLING

Have you ever been blinded?
Not by pain and suffering
Blinded by unwillingness
Unwilling to end my sinfulness
My heart misguided, senseless
Blinded by selfishness
Ignoring anyone else

Being driven by despair
My heart trapped in a corner
Losing more and more clarity
Perceiving hurt only one-sidedly

Have you ever been blinded by pride?
Losing yourself inside selfish heartache
Unwilling to admit fault or weakness
Stuck and unable to escape
Incapable to see another way
I need someone, something
to shake me . . . to wake me
Transform me from blind to blurry
From blurry to clarity

I had believed my problems could not change
I had believed that I cannot change
Will it always be this way?
Will I always be seen this way?
The truth is not in how I'm seen
The truth is a person
This person is Jesus
Only in God's redemption
Is there forgiveness and salvation in Christ
Revealed a new path to mend my heartache
Revealing my life is not a disastrous mistake
Actions that I'm now determined to take
To live in God's grace and changes God will make

CHAINS

I was living a life that was lost
This life I sought was like prison
Enslaved, confined without bars
I was bound and wrapped
A strait jacket of chains

Nobody built and forced this bond
Used to hold me captive
Self-inflicted captain-less ship
Tossed by storms and waves

I'm heading towards a rocky shore
I don't want this enslavement anymore
This life, these addictions such a chore
Destruction can't be my savior
My life is rotting to the core

I feel the temptation that won't let me be
I cry out to God, help is my plea
The undertow that's pulling, pulling me

Collapse in my life looming ahead
I pray to God remove this dread
Control in my life has disappeared
My heart with grief has been speared

I found freedom when I stopped fighting
Loosened the chains that I had tied around myself
Let go the chains used to imprison
A freed heart because of Christ
To Him I give my life of idolatry
To Him I give my life of being lost
Only in Christ is there forgiveness and salvation
Only in Christ the chains are gone
The chains used to hold me down

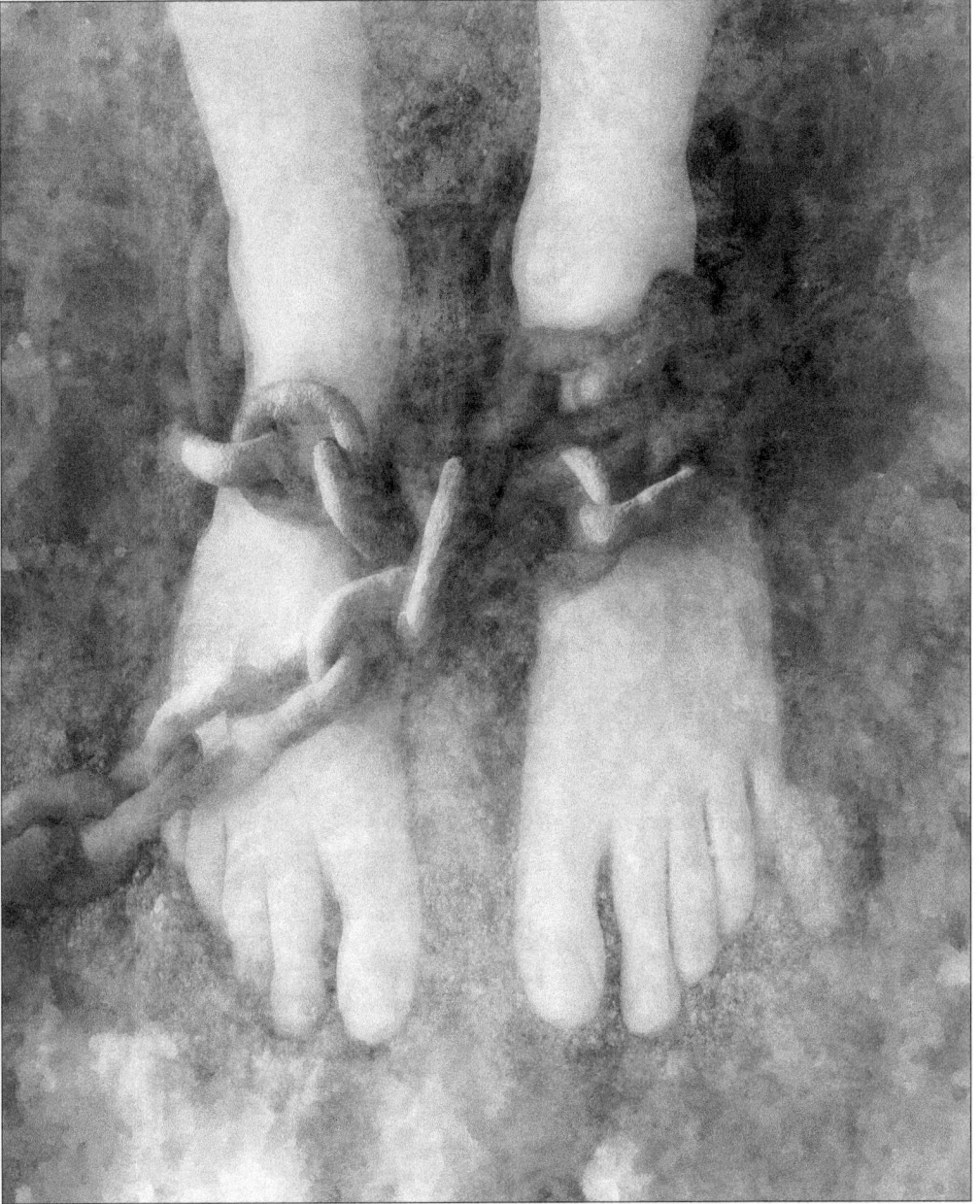

FORMED

The wise submit to refining
Changes in life through enduring trials
A process undertaken by all
Even in resistance to change

Hard cold steel
Shaped by fire
Hard cold heart
Shaped by fire

We aren't born this way
Being formed that is
Formation through pain
We aren't born this way
We need to be reborn

Though I too have endured fire
I did not ignite the flame myself
I did not possess the wisdom
To begin my flaming reformation

Plenty of fuel for the flame
It's time for the fire to grow
Don't let the flames get low
Into the fire idols to throw
My worship problems no one to blame

I've grown used to the heat
Only in flames will I become complete
These fiery trials make me reevaluate
What the desires of my heart are
And what should be thrown afar

Like iron been shaped by fire
A tool of God's grace
We aren't born this way
Having been shaped by fire
We are reborn through faith in Christ
God's grace so lavish

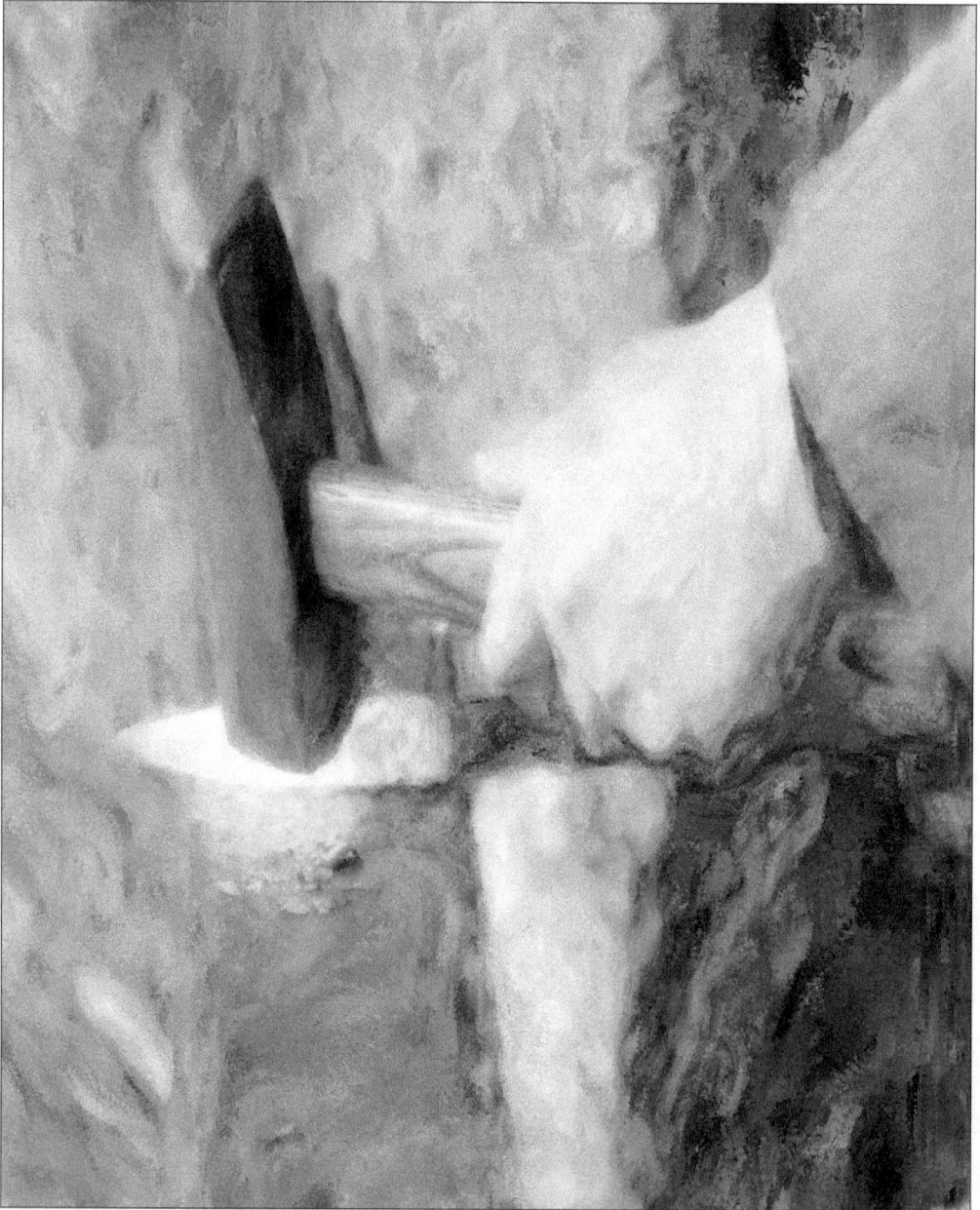

TWO WORLDS

Pulled in different directions but suspended
Desire for each, reduced and blended
My approach and desire need amended

I was stuck between two worlds
Because I was unwilling to let go

My heart pulled both ways
But somehow suspended
The worst of each world
This mixing and blending

As my life has unfolded
God awakened my heart, I realized
The wayward drift from side to side
Came from within, came from inside

Torn between two worlds, inside I was dying
Believing anything less would be lying
I traded in my old dying heart
It was exposed, needed a new start
It was God's grace that renewed my heart
No longer torn between two worlds
With a rebellious heart burned black
Salvation in Christ my heart has no lack

GRAVE

It's clear I lost my way
The lies, deceit, decay
I was aloof and astray

I was the architect of my own demise
Believing black lies of the unwise
Malice attempting to veil my pain
Unwilling to submit and avert

Now I know there is no one else to blame
I buried myself alive in my own grave
Beneath in my disgusting life of shame
I said yes to sinful things that enslave

Beneath with my lies knowing what I had become
Delusional thinking there was no way to escape
An ugly truth inside the lies, my heart was numb
My lonely dismal life gracious God undrape

There was another who was placed in a grave
This was not of His own but a willingness
I'm thankful He left this grave in a cave
God raised Christ from the grave to glory

Christ saved me from a life of death
Forgiveness and grace to save my life
In dying Jesus said finished in His final breath
Salvation in Christ peaceful eternal afterlife

WHISPER

Each decision begins to stack up
Living under the weight of my choices
I hardly recognize there being lines
Somewhere there stopped being lines at all
The whispers I chose to listen to

The subtle contradictions ignored
As compromise crept into my heart
A disregard of who I once was
The faith that I say I have
Oh, the whispers that entice
Slowly changing who I once was

Each whisper seemed so small
A slow sorrowful susurrous
When looked at by itself
It adds up to a lack of faith
All lines are gone in this whispering

Whispering voice of the flesh
The subtle contradictions
I allowed compromise to take hold
Forgetting the faith, I proclaim
Slowly changing to faithless

I once was close to truth
Blinded by faint deception
Conflict without opposition
Saying yes to all those whispers
In my pride in my hidden lies

Oh God, have mercy on me
I have failed You, weight in my heart
According to Your unfailing love
According to Your great compassion

Cancel out the guilt of my wrongdoings
I bring to You my Redeemer
A wayward selfish heart
In humility and desire to be Your servant
I know in Your Son Jesus
When I confess, You my gracious God
Always forgive, I'm so grateful!

TAKE

I took what I wanted regardless of You
I had to lose to know that I was wrong
Enslaving habits gone, now I can see
That You never left me alone
You gracious God are ever faithful

Loss can be a source of clarity
A taking away, a way for me to hide
Your Word oh God is always revealing

In Christ I choose to rebuild
Peace, love, and purpose in You
Nothing left to regret nothing left but hope

Take my brokenness, what remains
Now that I am free from the chains

Take my broken frame
Take what's left in me, renew me
No matter how much time it takes

I have only one path, one path
That path is with You my Savior
From emptiness You brought back life
From a broken heart I am revived
Take what's left of my life and create
Take what's left and rebuild

Lord, You had every reason to give up on me
Only You stood and waited as everyone departed
You carried me when I could only crawl
God will sustain me; I was never too far gone

FLOWERS OF GRASS

Emptiness owned my heart
Consumed all that I am
Living in a blinding mask
 A grasping for the wind

What I worshiped in my heart
What I truly desired
Drove everything I've done
Everything that can't be undone

In this emptiness it all means nothing
The grass withers, and the flower falls
A mere wisp of a vapor
Sadness and loneliness I embraced

Ensconced in broken promises
I am brokenness and scars
Like a life behind bars
A falling on a scimitar

Is this all the world can give?
Is broken emptiness anyway to live?
The chase for me is over I am finished

Inside my brokenness I cry out to You
Inside is my dismal desperate cry
Inside my darkness I'm ready to die
I'm tired of living with a blind eye
Living life just limping by

Oh, Jesus save, and rescue me
Save this wretched life is my decree
From my fallen brokenness I want to flee
Possible because You died for me on a tree

In Christ alone there is life
In Christ alone there is forgiveness
In Christ alone there is salvation
In Christ alone there is peace

SOJOURNER

My life has been a rough ride
Only You know my pain inside
Only You heard every time I cried
Only You saw every attempt to hide

You saw tears fall from my eyes
You saw my every compromise
You saw my life behind a guise
You saw my path, my demise

You're always loving, no one else could be
I turned my back on You
When I doubted, You stood by me
It's only Jesus that can rescue

I know that You are always there
No matter what's in my heart
Every moment in Your loving care
Even in the moments where I fell apart

I'm not ashamed to say the way I feel
I love You, You are my everything
In Christ I no longer desire to conceal
Within your mercy each day I can sing

I'm a sojourner in this place
Each day to live in Your grace
I don't have to be afraid anymore
My heart is Yours only You I adore

WITHOUT YOU

Today is another opportunity
Only God's love is loneliness immunity
I cannot survive today without You
All my efforts in my strength have failed
Again, today I cry out in need of You
Gracious Lord, restore strength in my heart

Even if You send me through trial of fire
I know it's for my benefit and not just a bonfire
Surrender to Your shaping my life something You require

Everything I am is because of You
My life my heart I give it all to You

In Your arms I am secure
In Your caring perfect ways
In Your perfect love so pure
Because of You peaceful are my days

Lord, I lay down what I want
No more pride to flaunt
Lord I lay down my life
I am nothing without You

DELUSION

How could I ever go back?
Back to living life in pitch black
Living life amongst the dead
Being enslaved in deepest dread

Inside my heart I know I could
I have no strength to say no
I would have forgotten Your grace
And become a slave to things so vile

How could I go back to live amongst the dead?
Delusions of what I thought was life, was real

Only Your love could set me free
Your call, Your grace would not let me be
In my heart I surrender to You
Loosen the bondage for my breakthrough

Oh God, I never want to leave Your arms
Only in You is there any real hope
In Christ, Your Grace, Your forgiveness
I confess that You Jesus are Lord

How could I go back to live amongst the dead?
Delusions of what I thought was life, was love
Now I have clear sight to see my path
Because for me You died peaceful aftermath
My former life, I have left everything behind
My heart and life to You are inclined

YOURS

You brought me into existence
Then a life I never thought could be
A life where eternity with You is real

You have shaped and are shaping my life
Knowing You has created love in my heart
I'm being reshaped by Your grace, Your truth
The perfection of Your love is true existence

I tried hard and so long to live a life of self
You reminded me of the failure of living for me
Your kingdom come Your will be done

I desired in my heart to follow a dream
You reminded me of the failure of my desires
Your kingdom come Your will be done
I tried in my own ways to battle enslavement
You reminded me of the failure of my strength
Like a dove in flight, I'm only free in Christ
Your kingdom come Your will be done

Yours Lord is the greatness and glory
I serve You Lord in Your kingdom
All praise, all glory to You
My God, My Savior, my life is Yours

LAMENT #2

The sound of silent voices
The call of destruction
Against my flagging weakness
That is my fallen flesh
Surveying me and my thoughts
It's sorrow and discontentment
A dark whispering loneliness
Succumb only to collapse
How long can I walk over graves?
In the cemetery of this fallen world
Searching for the tears of compassion
Yet find the frozen death of winter
Dead like the falling leaves
Lost hope of unchanging ways
My strength cannot survive or save
Am I unwilling or unable?
My desire has brought me only emptiness
The lust, the flesh, the pride of life
The barrenness of deception and lies
I know that I am guilty, oh God
I know that You look with loving mercy
Upon my wretched heart
In my confession You will forgive
Lord, reinstate me into Your purposes
I long for Your unfailing love and forgiveness
I plead with You oh God, help my faith in You
Only in Christ is there love and reconciliation
I'm so grateful that You forgive and cleanse
And restore me to Your loving heart

CONFESS

I wanted to worship You in my heart
I desired to give You my everything
I am weak, and I've failed You
It's actually worse than that
I've failed You so many times
I chose me over You again and again
How can I stand here before You?
I grasp for what I say is mine
That which only belongs to You
I am only able to bring You
Something that is already Yours

My God and my Savior I cry out to You
I confess my desire for self and how I ignore You
I am utterly ashamed, so ashamed
I confess that whatever I called my own
Lord, take what I am, take my broken remains
I offer to You my broken heart for You to heal
Your grace, forgiveness, and mercy so amazing to me
You laid down Your life when I refused to give You mine

UNTIL

Today in God's grace living in the not yet
From here to eternity the journey of life
Today can be a beginning to understanding
From here to eternity, we begin

I see who You are
Your Word oh God tells me
And who else can compare?
In my heart I meant what I said
I promised to stand and live for You
Lord, how am I doing in this promise?
Until the end, each day we begin
Until the end, that's where we begin

It is in our hearts that we choose
Define what has meaning in life
From the heart we step out in life
Lord continue to shape and change my heart
That my life is about and for You
Some will ask how this can be
That You can change my heart
I surrender to You Lord and Your ways
I choose Lord to follow You all my days

JOURNEY

The journey is arduous
Traveled so far to find so little
The struggle has been nocuous
Resulting in a heart that is brittle

Is there meaning in suffering?
Is there meaning in tragedy?
Oh God shelter me I need covering
Oh God please end this agony

In the search for meaning
Dark clouds have led me here
I need Your grace intervening
My need of You my God so severe

Seeking the world, I have been taught a lie
Guidance has been wrong this whole time
All I did was agree and comply
I ignored You, but Your grace is sublime

I was compelled to continue the fight
Confined in the trappings of desired freedom
Alone and angry I would cry at night
My life of lies and deception, I'm done

Fighting battles I could not win
I'm ready to learn from my mistakes
I hate to think what could have been
It's been a life of sin and heartaches

I need You Jesus, Your forgiveness, I'm so lost
My heart so desperately needs to be changed
My sin and rebellion I'm learning how much it cost
From You, I no longer can stand to be estranged

NIGHTS SO DARK

I have felt alone for so long
Choosing to live with darkness
Inside knowing my choices are wrong
Gripped by fear and selfishness my inertness

Yearning for love became countless nights
That buried my weary and hard heart
Enslaved to destructive habits, an ugly sight
The endless cycle of fleshly desire ripping me apart

But you Jesus brought an end to this life of death
And brough love and grace to a calloused life
Loosened the grip of sin, can now take a breath
I can look ahead in Christ without a life of strife

Hold me in Your loving arms
Carry me through the darkest valley
In Christ I can now endure without alarm
My life no longer a dark scary alley

I can still remember the day I realized
The way You drew me, Your love
I could finally see how I had compromised
Forgetting what's left behind, in You I'm in awe of

With a deep sigh of peace
I can face tomorrow
I must decrease so You can increase
I pray that my love for You will continue to grow

REFLECT

Many nights I wondered what's before me
Trying to unravel my heart from the grip of fear
I still have nights where I pray and plea
In those moments now I know Jesus is near

Being alone was stale hollow air
Enveloped in streams of uncertainty
How much fearful loneliness can I bear?
In those moments I seek Jesus fervently

I feel temptation collapsing upon my mind
Mistakes of the past, waves of guilt and shame
The accuser says by my failures I am defined
God's lavish grace in Christ, I'm no longer the same

My battered bones tried to endure the fight
Against the endless ocean of sin and accusation
All my sin and rebellion has come to light
Forgiveness, mercy, and grace in Christ not damnation

THAT DAY

I remember that day so long ago
It's like a din in the background of my life
It's always there and making the same claims
On my life that it did that day
That day rides on top of all the other mistakes and
failures in my life
That day continues to float to the top
To be a stain on the wall of my life
I try to paint it over, to cover it, to make it disappear
It bleeds through my dismal attempt to cover
To distance myself, to deny that day
Can I gain a perspective and learn from that day?
Is this a way to seed future growth and healing?
Is there any real hope in character traits and other
successes in my life?
To recover from failure is change possible?
My attempts to change, were just another layer of
shark gray paint
Trying to cover the stain of that day
That shark gray paint has a stain bleeding through
Laughing at my pathetic attempt to distance, to
cover to make amends.

That day has a voice, a very familiar voice

A voice that says things to me, things it knows will
produce an effect
It's very effective in producing the intended results
That voice that says I am a failure, a loser, a waste of time
It says I am worthless, hideous, a disgrace
My past, it's like looking into a cold fog with dark shadows
Lurking and accusing, A dark and swirling tempest
Gazing into that accusing mist, I feel lonely
That cold fog descending upon my heart to block
the view to truth

To keep me in its grasp, that day wants to own me
It has owned me for a very long time
The cold grip of merciless accusations
Spears of hatred that pierce my heart
Suffocating emptiness
Abysmal miasma
My broken heart has been bleeding out
Bleeding over the pain and anguish of shame and guilt

My life is a frozen tundra battered by the icy blast north wind
Endless winter that is draining, draining me
A barren branch in winter wearing a sweater of frost
Within the cold grip of death, a valley of ghastly misery
Hate tattooed on my knuckles
The inescapable reality of my heart
A dying sun suffering remorse and regret

I could have stayed harboring my anguish on shore
I chose instead to expose and sink to the ocean floor
I needed to, I can't live this way anymore
I feel as though I'm drowning
The murky waters are so cold
I feel stuck in a place I hate
It's a tide of gloom and self-loathing
I walk through my life with a limp
As I continue to drag a ball and chain
It's been many years and more tears
Look at this mess I call life
I have been searching to find answers and peace in my life
I see that times are getting harder and darker
The voice of that days proclaims that I was born to
lose and destined to fail
That there is no peace in life to be had for me
All I have is shame, guilt, failure, and disgrace
The voice continues to run me down and claim its
ownership of my life

Suffering has been my daily lot for too long

It's difficult to share the shame of that day with anyone
I fear the exposure of that day of reckoning
Does God care about the troubles, the pain, the
suffering in my life?
God, I need you, I'm a disgusting broken mess
In my pain and misery, I finally cried out to God
Oh God rescue me from this agony of a life of guilt and hatred
Oh God shelter me from the gripping talons of vile
things I said yes to
Lord help me move beyond my self-loathing and
my hatred of that day
God, I'm so broken I have great fatigue of being morose
Lord help me to trust, and have faith in You Holy God
I confess my sins of that day against You
Forgive my wretched acts and wayward weary heart
Lord take shards of my life and make me whole

This work to redeem, to make things right is the work of God
The work to redeem lost and broken lives like mine
Redemption and salvation by no other name than Jesus
God is the one who brings all things to account
Including every deep shameful and hidden thing
As Jesus discerns the thoughts and intents of my heart
He might discover that my desires to bring others to
account are not altogether pure
I, like many love the idea of God bringing others to account
I don't love the idea when it's me
Being pierced, and evaluated between the joints and beyond the marrow
I needed to confess my part in that day, God made that clear
I did, I confessed my sins against God
Confessed Jesus Christ as Lord and Savior
God saved and rescued a dismal failure
I now pray about that day and God
I'm ready to forgive those involved that day
In perfect timing God will make all things right
In Christ I am also now at peace with that day
In God's plan to redeem me, I am free
Free from the shackles of sin, guilt, and regret

In Christ I can finally forgive
Jesus forgives my sins, now in His strength
I can do the same, forgive what I thought was unforgivable
Looking back on that day, now instead of anger, bitterness, hatred
It causes me to fall on the grace and mercy of God
In my prayer of desperation, You my Savior are faithful
I am so thankful that God is merciful and gracious
Leaning on God's grace and mercy helps me understand
That it is God who calls us and all things into account
God is good, loving, and compassionate, He is my
good, good Father!

STRUGGLE

In my life through struggle have I found You
I chose rebellion and relented to surrender to You
You never forsook me, You are always true
May Your hands now shape me like clay

I have begun to understand Your love
Hollow out this life so it can be a light
All my sin and rebellion against You disposed of
I'm no longer living against You in sin and spite

Only through struggle have I found rest
Only in surrender to Christ is there any hope
You my Savior and Lord I'm so blessed
I no longer feel like my life is on a tightrope

Lord, remove from me any wicked way
The deception that trapped me is gone
May my life be Yours and for Your display
It's You and Your grace that I can count on

MORNING

All along it was me who needed to be changed
Each morning now awaits in worship of You
All along it was me, from You to be rearranged
Each day now I know You will carry me through

What I have left behind does not matter
All that matters is what I give is all to You
No longer a life of cloak and dagger
I am Yours and stick with You like glue

I have seen stars fall, the sun rise
You are all that is worth living for
You saw my misery and heard my cries
My life is about You more and more

You are all that is worthy
You are always with me by my side
I praise You for Your grace and mercy
I give to You my Savior all my sinful pride

WORTH

This world was never worth the effort
Corruption crawled from its hideous carcass
Living for my desires in a hostile desert
I cared about me saying no to You on purpose

Like the dead rising from an open grave
Lies of splendor and tongues of deceit
Saying yes to loathsome things, I was a knave
All along it was a living in death, defeat

I was gasping for my last breath
I can hide no longer there's nothing left
I was in darkness and yearning for death
Saying yes to all the lies I was bereft

All my sorrows have led me here
As I cry out to You in my misery
I want my life of sin to disappear
I cry out to You Holy God hear my inquiry

As I reflect not on me and my sin
But reflect on You and Your majesty
I need You so new life can begin
Help me to see my sin and depravity

 I confess how I have failed You
My merciful God and my Savior
My life of rebellion I'm through
Only in Your forgiveness new behavior

Forgive this wayward life of disregard
Lord, enter my heart and change the decay
Heal my weary heart that is scarred
Life in Christ my Savior a new birthday

TURN

I've looked straight into the eyes
The eyes of evil darkness and destruction
Lusting and wanting each day a part of me dies
I continued to ignore and despise Your instruction

I turned my head again and again
Unwilling to leave the cave of the depraved
I had no desire to say no to abstain
Ensconced in my desire and so enslaved

The fate of those who trust in liars
Reprobates miserable alone and afraid
Trapped and in the grip like locking pliers
From You gracious God I greatly strayed

In what I chose You are the One I left behind
I will no longer say yes to sin and turn my head
No more earthly desires to live as though blind
In Your grace and love, I have lost my sense of dread

Earthly desires now left for dead
End the chase of this worldly dream
Saved because Christ died and bled
You my Savior are glorious and supreme

My selfishness and desires consumed me
Lord, forgive the days that I erased Your name
I'm thankful You heard my desperate plea
I live now for Christ Jesus and His fame

WATCH

You were always there and watching
As I chose sin and nearly destroyed myself
What I chose and did was a life of botching
Living as though life is a thing-in-itself

I lived for me, and You I betrayed
The wanting for nothing more than comfort
My utter shame and disgrace displayed
I lived in disregard; of You I fell short

Only Jesus would die for me as sacrifice
Your love, only Yours is a love that saves
Jesus' death for sinners has paid the price
Your love and forgiveness no longer sin slaves

You Lord have stood by me in grace
I was a coward and a rebel I went astray
Because of You I no longer live in sin and disgrace
The cost of sin, Lord You were willing to pay

HESITATE

The human heart is a scary thing
It can both break and be broken
In my head I'll say forget about it
Knowing that I'll get hurt and regret it
Ask me now and I will hesitate

Many boats never leave the dock
I believe there comes a time when they should
If you ask now to see my heart
I know I will hesitate

In my heart I'm fearful of many things
I'm the kind that tends to contemplate
The kind that tends to hesitate
What came with You Lord was a view to admire
I feel like now in Your grace I can aspire

Thinking about it long and hard today
I realized I was unwilling to live Your way
My choices should have been better
My life is now Yours, an open letter

Lord, ask me now and I won't hesitate
I love You, I live and fall for You
You first loved me, there's no debate
Your love and compassion always come through

BREAK

I woke up this morning and heard the news
That familiar feeling, I know the pain of a heartbreak
This is simply more than a case of Monday blues
I don't have answers, I'm confused, nothing to fake

This life isn't easy, this life isn't always clear
I'm feeling desperate, I'm so in need, I need Jesus
I don't want to live any longer with fear
Jesus, I need Your love, much to discuss

I've had questions and doubts before
When I have upped and walked away
Not looking to You and going out the door
Because of You by my side now I can stay

When life is hard, and my heart is about to break
I no longer doubt and yearn to know why
I cry out to You and Your grace partake
I know You will never leave me high and dry

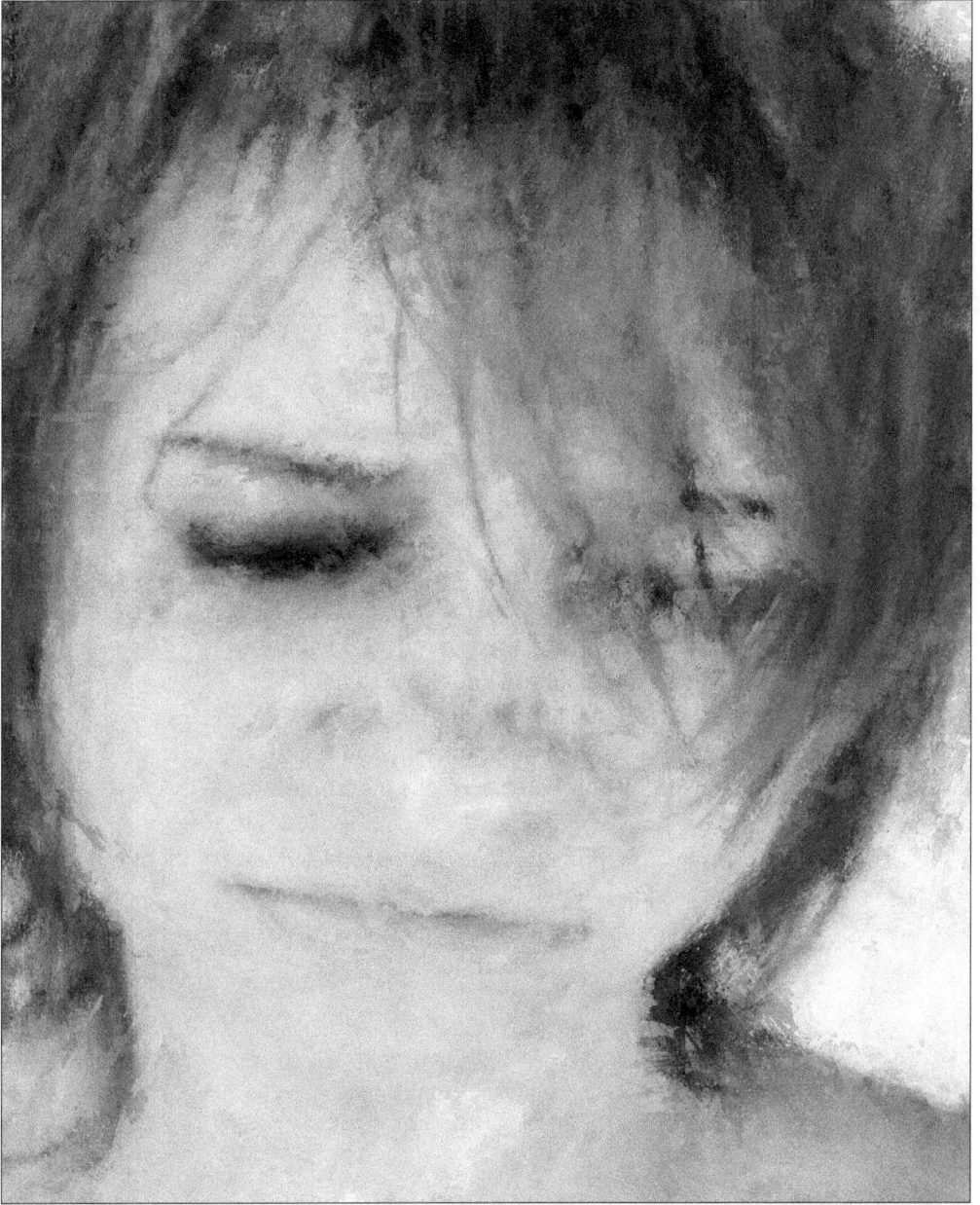

FAINT

Sins can be like stones, they sink in
Like breathing in air
You can keep them inside, for a while
Hurt and pain will persist if allowed
Our hearts can be barricaded
Scars from the battle will adorn
I want to know love that is real
True love is a person
True love is Jesus Christ
Lord, I want to be like You
Please, show me the way
I want to hear You call my name
In the end and say well done faithful servant

I need help in not looking back
The indulgences of this world are faint lights
All they did was leave me stranded and lost
Desperate reaching through pockets with holes
I was stubborn and put up a fight
That battle surely took its toll
Lord please awake my soul
Only You Lord can make me whole

When the pressure is on, I used to feel alone
Once again trapped inside my thoughts and fear
Now because of Your truth and grace I've grown
Who You are Lord to me is so dear

LIVE

I love You more than words can say
There used to be tears on my pillowcase
No longer do I see the skies as gray
You Lord paid for my sins, died in my place

Only one thing matters in this life You gave
Will I live for You before the other side?
To live for You and tell how only You can save
Salvation in Christ because for us You died

I had put my faith in man-made gods
Pursuit of the world only left me blind
I desired the limelight, with You I was at odds
Struggling in self worship was a grind

Many ask, have you ever experienced true love?
Do you know what it's made of?
I know where it's coming from
Jesus the only person where true love can come

ROSE

Red roses are beautiful flowers
I love the intricate design of the petals
The deep red color reminds me
Of my sin that Jesus bled and died for
The fragrance of a rose is sublime
If redemption has a fragrance
It's as sweet as a rose
A rose also reminds me
Of all the anguish and despair
Of the trials and sorrows
Of the sadness and tears
Of the brokenness of this fallen world
Of all the hardships and problems, we face
Every thorn has a rose
Every pain is not in vain
God will never leave or forsake me
As a child of God, I'm never alone
I can endure every thorn of this life
Because I know my Savior lives!

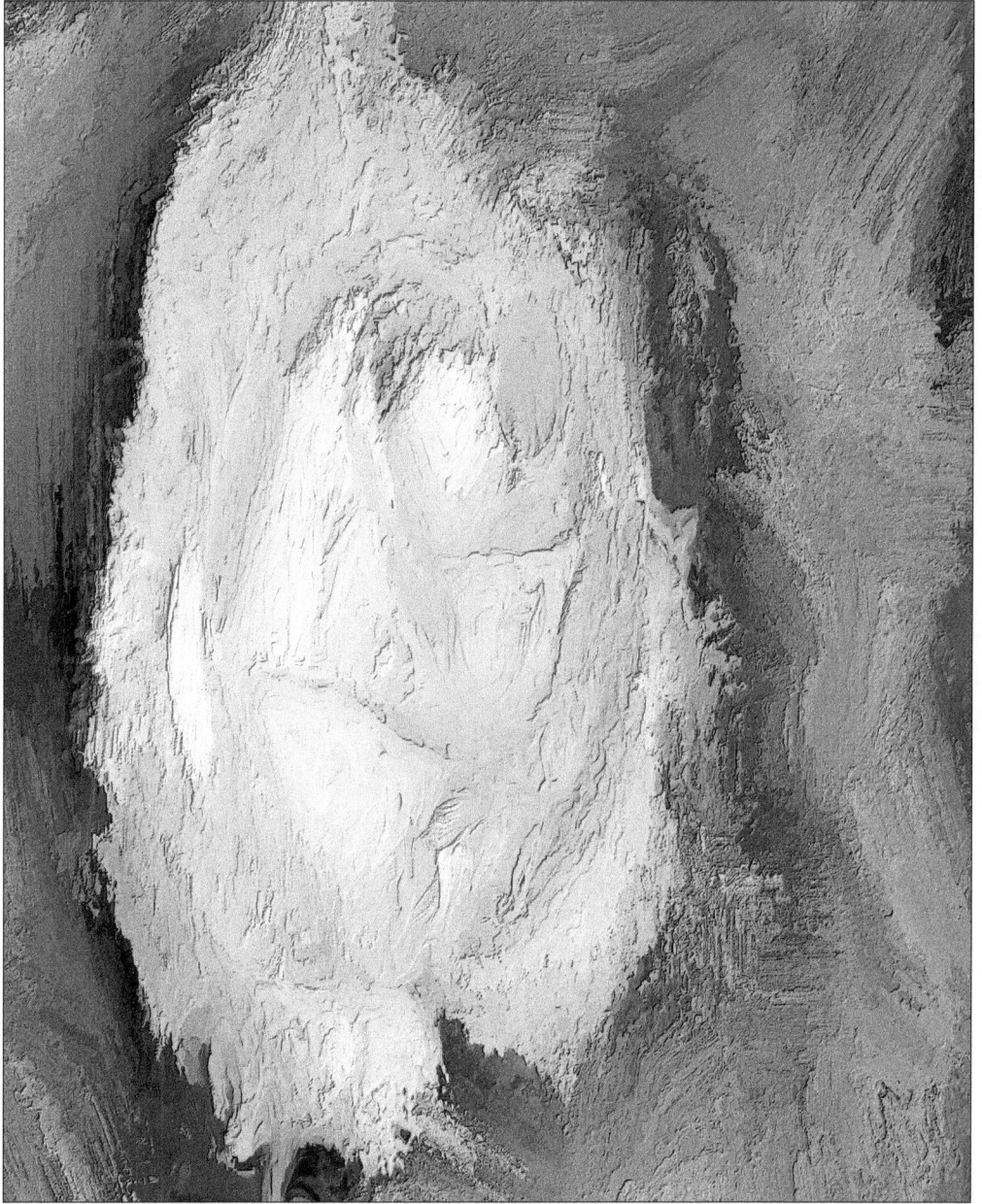

www.ingramcontent.com/pod-product-compliance
Lightning Source LLC
LaVergne TN
LVHW021615080426
835510LV00019B/2581